No Mo' Explainin'

Keisha Y. Lapsley

No Mo' Explainin'

Copyright © 2020 by Keisha Y. Lapsley

All rights reserved. No part of this book may be reproduced or transmitted in any form or by any means without written permission of the author. All rights reserved. Except for use in the case of brief quotations embodied in critical articles and reviews, the reproduction or utilization of this work in whole or part in any form by any electronic, digital, mechanical or other means, known or hereafter invented, including xerography, photocopying, scanning, recording, or any information storage or retrieval system, is forbidden without prior written permission of the author and publisher.

The scanning, uploading, and distribution of this book via internet or via any other means without permission of the publisher and author is illegal and punishable by law. Purchase only authorized versions of this book and do not participate in or encourage electronic piracy of copyrighted materials.

For ordering, booking, permission, or questions, contact the author please visit www.authorklap.com or email at keycitypro@gmail.com

ISBN: 978-0-9995314-7-1

Publisher: KeyCity Publishing

Cover Design: Simone Bryant of It Takes Faith Productions

This book is dedicated to the multifaceted ideology of people who won't take the time to understand African Americans and people of color outside of the societal schism and stereotypical truism perpetuated by history, media, entertainment, and politics. How much more explaining must be done for those who choose to remain consciously and sincerely ignorant to understand that humanity is not defined by color but creation? When it comes to our lives, there must be a conversation from the (4) P's of society (pulpit, police, politics, and president) about the original sin (racism) embedded in this country's history towards us; and, to this present day from the founding fathers to the future of this nation, recognizing the validity of black folk as EQUAL! The current conflicts we face today from the Revolutionary War of 1775 to the future of this nation, the American flag is saturated in just as much of African American blood as any other citizen. Yet, we are told we are unpatriotic if we don't stand for the flag, put your hand over your heart, sing the national anthem regardless of the 3rd stanza, or just comply with the police regardless of the video as if we are here on credit with no dues paid. Some people only want to hear their own voice and the lies this nation has indoctrinated its people into believing that OUR LIVES DON'T MATTER AS MUCH! NO MO EXPLAININ'! – Douglas Lapsley

Acknowledgments

I haven't done acknowledgments in my books for a long time, but if there is a time for acknowledgments right now, this is it!

First and foremost, I want to thank my Father in heaven for giving me what to do with all the anger, hurt, and disappointment I presently feel in regards to all that is going on in our nation and to the ones (nonblack) who I never would have thought would be the ones that I'd have to write off. It is because of I AM that I'm writing this book. I didn't know what to do with all this anger, and He clearly said, "Write! Do what you do best, write," and that is what I'm doing right now.

Thank you to our brothers and sisters (black and nonblack alike) in the fight for equality, justice, and change. Your strategic planning and influential voices are ringing throughout this world. Keep going! Keep pressing! No one knows what you are going through behind the scenes (which I'm sure is far more than what we see), but God does, and I continually pray for your protection.

Thank you to our nonblack brothers and sisters who are willing to learn and understand about our struggles and our fight, educating your family and friends (even amid pushback), protesting with us, working with us to change the laws so we may have fair justice, and standing with us. We see you! We thank you! We salute you!

Thank you to the good cops, law enforcement, and officials who have endured ugly and cruel behavior due to the corrupt police, law enforcement, and officials and stand up against them. You sacrifice your lives daily, and it's because you want to, not because you have to, and that sacrifice isn't taken lightly.

THANK YOU!!!

Table of Contents

The Preliminary 1
Shoe Mileage 4
Starting with the Flag 8
Knee Reasons 13
You Wouldn't Defend Me 15
You Still Think It's About George Floyd 21
Sayings & Explanations 30
I Will Not Fear 34
Be Careful Dear #UrRacismIsShowing 38
Stop Lying!!! 41
Story Time 46
No Mo' Explainin'! 59

The Preliminary

The question I get the most is, "Where did this book come from?" My answer is simple, anger. It was a must for me to pray about everything that was going on because it weighed on me heavily. I stayed quiet for a while because if I said anything at that time, there's no telling what would have come out my mouth. Anger taunted me. Frustration gripped me. Thoughts flooded my mind, and the ignorance of people's racist comments took all that to a whole new level.

I'm sure you really don't know what to expect from this book. You're not sure if the words you read will be from an angry person. If you guess that, you'd be right! Where does that anger come from, and how can we, as a people, help defuse that anger?

The anger comes from a place of rejection, a system that's built to keep us enslaved and down, lies, manipulation, and the slaughtered past of my ancestors. No, I wasn't a slave. No, I didn't grow up around slave masters. However, I did grow up watching the KKK march down the street, unbothered on my TV as a child. I grew up watching how white people interacted with my parents. I watched how I couldn't go into a store without being followed around. I saw how the color of my skin intimidated Caucasians. I heard how I was called out of my name because of the color of my skin. I experienced negative racial situations on numerous occasions, at college, church, middle school, high school, and other places.

Since I was a child raised in Atlanta then moved to Indianapolis, I was on guard when it came to white people. The reason I was on the defense was because from what I saw in Atlanta from some of them was generally hostile. I saw what they were doing to black people. I watched how they acted towards us and listened to the hateful words they said. When we moved to Indianapolis, I wasn't sure how to handle being around Caucasians. I tiptoed carefully and sized them up. Eventually, I knew who I was okay with and who I wasn't. Being on guard tends to make you mean and angry. That was me; I was her. I felt safer around my people. Growing up, I couldn't shake the memory of what I saw in Atlanta. Don't get me wrong, it wasn't all white people. Even that shouldn't have to be said, but since we're here…there we are. I did not know who I could trust, but I knew I could believe in the lies that were taught and our history that wasn't explained. I knew me and people like me were considered different, and we are hated for it.

The Preliminary

FIGHT FOR BREONNA TAYLOR!
SHE'S NOT HERE TO FIGHT FOR HERSELF!
ARREST AND CHARGE THE COPS RESPONSIBLE FOR HER DEATH!

Shoe Mileage

Walk

Walk

Walk…a mile in our shoes

I've picked up and put down this pen more than I can count

I got more anger in me than Tyler Perry got in his bank account

But I'm also deeply saddened and hurt

Due to the reasons why our brothers and sisters lie 6 ft deep in the dirt

It's because they don't want us to stand up on our feet

Nor to feed on our black history on which we feast

But want us to ride with their history while ours take a backseat

Yet we rise while their engrained lies decrease

Let this be written in concrete

To every racist, you are sitting in the hot seat

And to those who aren't racist but stay silent and retreat

You can't just close your eyes and press delete

It's time for you to change shoes and put some mileage on your feet

Because there aren't any work hours recorded on your timesheet

Just for a second close your eyes

Open your ears and listen attentively to our cries

Shoe Mileage

Let's trade shoes for a sec and see what applies
And while we're there expose the systematic lies
Trade your privilege for our persecution
Trade our problems for your solutions
Put on our punishment for your protection

Trade your opportunities for our oppression
Trade-in your safety and take on our survival
From the time the land was stolen until the time of our arrival
Trade your lies for our truth, your peace for our war, and your power for our position
Because we are sick and tired of our people's bodies being taken to the mortician
Walk
Walk
Walk
Walk a mile in our shoes and ask yourself, would you still function the same way as you do now, or would you walk without judgment and with understanding because of the

different shoes you decided to wear and put your hands to the plow?
You won't know until…you
Walk
Walk
Walk

Fight for Breonna Taylor!

Arrest her murderers right now!

Starting with the Flag

A few of the many words I hear ringing out on interviews through radio, television, and or podcasts across the nation is, "My great-grandfather, my grandfather, or my father died representing that flag." How many of you listened to those very same words? Sounds patriotic, doesn't it? Upon hearing those words makes you want to stand to your feet and sing the National Anthem, doesn't it? However, there are follow-up actions I never see, and that is justice for people of color; at least the justice we don't have to fight for to receive said justice.

The good 'ole American flag was created on June 14, 1777. Later in 1897, laws were put in place regarding the protection of the flag. It was meant for voluntary compliance. The laws stated that marking on the flag for any reason, using it for marketing or advertising, defiling, or mutilating it by words or through action was prohibited. Under the model flag desecration law, the term "flag" was defined to include any flag, standard, ensign, or color, or any representation of such made of any substance whatsoever and of any size that evidently purported to be said flag or a picture or likeness thereof, upon which shall be shown the colors, the stars, and stripes in any number, or the person seeing the same without deliberation may believe the same to represent the flag of the U.S. However, in 1968, it was made illegal by federal law to "knowingly" cast "contempt" upon "any flag of the United States by publicly mutilating, defacing, defiling, burning or trampling upon it." (Independence Hall Association, 1995)

I find it ironic the same law that says it is a federal crime to deface, defile, burn, or trample the flag for commercial, political, or other purposes does not extend that same ferocious tenacity and courtesy towards black people. I find it even more deplorable, after learning, segregation within the military (which your family died for) didn't end until 1953, that's the same time some of our parents were born (for those of us in our 40's)! This wasn't that long ago. Please take a second glance at that last statement. Our people were fighting alongside your people and was STILL not honored as equal men, was not allowed to eat with the men in your family, or use the same restrooms, or bunk with them. Again, please tell me more of why you honor the flag more than the people that the flag is supposed to represent!

Keisha Y. Lapsley

I'm appalled this has to be said, but it wasn't just YOUR great-great grandfather, great grandfather, grandfather, and father who served in the military; it was OURS too! But ours came with a hell of a whole lot more blood! How is that so? History tells us and shown us, and some lived it, and some of us are still living in the results of it. The years between the 18th and early 20th centuries, our people fought for the lives of everyone only to return home for no one to fight for them. They still had no rights, no proper medical care, unequal pay, was still in fear of being kidnapped and returned to slavery (because even though it was ruled illegal in the 1700s, slavery picked back up in the early 1800s). While they served on those very same front lines you're so proud of, they served with markings of whips on their backs, loss of their children due to being sold or taken to someone else or killed, the rape and the defilement of their wives, sisters, and mothers, the burning flesh of their neighbor, brother, sister, father, or mother, and even being rape victims themselves.

Please tell me again why you are so proud to protect the flag that doesn't protect all? Tell me how the flag has more laws in place for it than the "free" citizens of that flag. Tell me why we should be quiet and not protest to receive what the flag is supposed to represent. If you cannot answer those questions with honesty,

Starting with the Flag

then please stop telling us about how your family died for that flag and how you hold it in high regard.

FIGHT FOR
BREONNA TAYLOR!
SHE'S NOT HERE TO FIGHT FOR
HERSELF!
ARREST AND CHARGE THE COPS
RESPONSIBLE FOR HER DEATH!

Knee Reasons

No! Stand up! You can't protest that way!

Get up horse and run like we're paying you to do and do that on another day

You have no right to disrespect our flag!

My grandfather served America, you brag

We're wanted to pledge our allegiance to a flag

Yet, your words come with a hefty price tag

The last lines in the allegiance don't seem to describe America at all

Our own words ensnare us, United we stand, divided we fall

That same flag says we, America, are indivisible

If we were in court, I'd have evidence that would make that statement inadmissible

After over 400 years, African Americans are still treated with divisibility

Along with hostility, humility, and hardly ever civility

Liberty is mentioned, meaning being free from oppressive restrictions imposed by authority

Now look back over the years and tell me how this applies to minorities

Then it has the nerve to say justice for all

Keisha Y. Lapsley

Uh oh, stop it now cause we done hit a curveball
Now it's time to take a knee
Somebody go get Kermit cause it's time for some tea
You keep mentioning the flag and as an American, you should
Just be sure to keep that same energy when it infringes on a fellow American's livelihood
You fight for a flag but don't fight for the one next to you
Yet, they are the same ones that would be down for you
How is it that a knee to the neck is accepted?
But a peaceful kneeling is rejected?
You not mad about the kneeling because of the flag
You mad cause you have to face the truth about our hashtags
You not even mad cause of your loved ones who served
You mad cause your blind lies are no longer preserved
You angry at the knee cause now you will have to observe
The truth of the injustice that has been submerged
Take a Knee…

You Wouldn't Defend Me

Dear Use to be "Friends,"

You know, it's sad that I can't even start with a happy and genuine greeting or salutation because of the deep-seated hurt I feel. Out of all the people, I never expected it to be ya'll. In case you didn't know, the dismissal of my people means the complete dismissal of me. I'm shocked and disgusted you would use the words you use, crack jokes, and talk about my people and think I wouldn't feel some type of way about it. When going through my social media feeds, to see what you post and have commented leaves my heart broken. We shared time together, brought our families together, hung out together, worked together, shared laughs, and rough times together...bruh...I mean, I let you in my house around my family only to find out that this is how you feel about me?!??!!

There is no way this friendship could be mended or maintained after this because I don't trust you unless you are adamite about understanding and seeing it from more than just your view. I wouldn't call you racist, but I will say you don't believe in the African American cause or fight for injustice. Since you do not believe in that then you don't believe the reasons behind it, nor our pain because from what I can see, you're good as long as we sit down and shut up. I wouldn't be able to get pass your hurtful words and what's more the language and comments you've allowed others to get away without correction. Trust is a very fickle thing, hard to come by and easy to lose. You embodied what friendship means to me, and I think that's what hurt worse. It's not that we couldn't laugh together because whenever we came together, it was always fun, but it's the realization if something went down, you wouldn't defend me (even if the truth of the situation stared you smack in the face). My husband and I allowed you around our most treasured possessions, our children, and even had them in your company by yourselves. Whew! Lawd! Now, I know if something happened, you wouldn't protect them, and you would find every reason and excuse to back the other "player" or should I just say the police. I'm trying to tell you —God was with you because if something happened and we found out then what we know now, there ain't a blockade that would have withheld the freight train that was sure to come.

I don't choose to walk away from this friendship because of your opinion. I choose to walk away because of the ignorance of your opinion, and your unwillingness to see this from all sides. You only see it from one side, yours, which makes you close-minded and one dimensional (no matter how you try to make it seem like you're open-minded). I walk away because even after knowing me, you still choose to believe lies or half-truths about black people. I choose to walk away because of your words and your heart and calling us low self-esteemed victims with the mentality of Islamic terrorists. What?! Yes! You align us with terrorists but don't align your very own people as terrorists by the things they have done in the past and what they still do to this day. You even referred to us as "these people" in a derogatory tone, nor did you correct others when they used the same words. They agreed with you, so I don't expect anything more from you. I am disappointed, however, because you seem to feel like we are saying treat us special, but if you think us asking to be treated like human

> **I choose to walk away because I choose Me**

beings is being treated special, then you, especially, are part of the problem. I walk away because you show me what you believe every time you post something counterproductive to our fight. Do you know why the fight against crooked law enforcement is huge? The fight is serious because they get justice and the ones, they kill does not because of the shield they wear. If we were receiving justice, it wouldn't be an issue. You still have no clue why we protest. WE – ARE – NOT – RECEIVING – JUSTICE!!! Plain and simple!

The fact we must protest, fight, lift our voices, raise all kinds of hell, and continuously say Black Lives Matter should tell you why we're frustrated. Y'all were okay as long as we stayed quiet, being the good "house negros." Meanwhile, you are silently quiet about the lives of black men and women being taken to the morgue by the thousands, silent about being beat with batons and attacked by police dogs, fire hoses being let loose on us, knees on our necks, shot in the back, etc…etc…etc. See, I'm already tired of explaining. We are just trying to get justice. As for the riots and looting, no, I don't condone it, but even you erupt and go off on people when you're fed up, so how do you think we feel after 400 plus years of the same thing? You can barely handle a one-time heated situation without losing your mind, but you expect us to just go along? GTMOH!! On top of that, some of those who started the riots were agitators and paid to infiltrate the peaceful protest. Still, you don't mention that when you say, "they" or "them" or "those people." You don't mention the black Americans that you so casually dismiss as "them" or "they" or "those people" when they protest peacefully, help those who have been harmed, protected police officers, shook hands and gave hugs to the cops and a mountainous of other great things black people have done.

What's heartbreaking is using the Bible to back your ignorance. I wonder, if you really listened to the Holy Spirit, would you be willing to hear his point of view? What if I shared with you Joshua 1:14-15, "Your wives, your children, and your livestock may stay in the land that Moses gave you east of the Jordan, but all your fighting men, ready for battle, just cross over ahead of your fellow Israelites. You are to help them until the LORD gives them rest, as he has done for you, and until they too have taken possession of the land the LORD your God is giving them. After that, you may go back to and occupy your own land, which Moses the servant of the LORD gave you east of the Jordan toward the sunrise." What did you see after reading those scriptures? I'll share what I received. It meant some fellow brothers and sisters do not have rest, nor have they received the land *THE LORD* wants them to have. He's telling the ones who have collected their portion to fight with those who haven't obtained theirs. Is that so hard to understand? It was GOD who gave these instructions. We, African Americans, have not received our portion nor any land. We can't even get justice!!! He didn't call for you to become the same as those who oppress us and keeps us from our portion and our land; He called you to fight with us, so we all can rest! Remember, you may be resting now, but war may knock at your own door soon.

I've never seen a peaceful war and make no mistake, we're at war for justice! At some point, we all face a battle. Don't leave the same brothers and sisters behind who have and will fight for you because you could end up fighting your battle alone. Their eyes, ears, and heart may be shut to your struggle due to how you treated them during theirs.

Consequently, it is because of these things you have said and done is why I know you'd NEVER defend me or people who look like me, which is why I must walk away. It hurts me to my core that you'd find every excuse to discredit me and make me out to be the villain even though you know me and my character. You are the reason we must fight for justice because of your injustice towards me and those who look like me.
- Goodbye "Friends"

You Wouldn't Defend Me

You Still Think It's About George Floyd

Let's start with this first, it just ain't about George Floyd. For the world, it's about George Floyd because they finally see what the black community has been talking about all these years, but for us, George Floyd is the "Ain't No Way We Can Let This Continue!"

It's About…

1st Murder	2nd Murder	3rd Murder
4th Murder	5th Murder	6th Murder
7th Murder	8th Murder	9th Murder
10th Murder	11th Murder	12th Murder
13th Murder	14th Murder	15th Murder
16th Murder	17th Murder	18th Murder
19th Murder	20th Murder	21st Murder
22nd Murder	23rd Murder	24th Murder
25th Murder	24th Murder	26th Murder

ARE YOU TIRED OF READING MURDER YET?

27th Murder	28th Murder	29th Murder

You Still Think It's About George Floyd

30th Murder	31st Murder	32nd Murder
33rd Murder	34th Murder	35th Murder
36th Murder	37th Murder	38th Murder
39th Murder	40th Murder	41st Murder
42nd Murder	43rd Murder	44th Murder
45th Murder	46th Murder	47th Murder
48th Murder	49th Murder	50th Murder
51st Murder	52nd Murder	53rd Murder
54th Murder	55th Murder	56th Murder
57th Murder	58th Murder	59th Murder
60th Murder	61st Murder	62nd Murder
63rd Murder	64th Murder	65th Murder

ARE YOU TIRED OF READING MURDER YET? DOES IT SEEM POINTLESS? IF IT SEEMS POINTLESS THEN YOU DEEM ALL THESE LIVES POINTLESS.

66th Murder	67th Murder	68th Murder
69th Murder	70th Murder	71st Murder
72nd Murder	73rd Murder	74th Murder
75th Murder	76th Murder	77th Murder
78th Murder	79th Murder	80th Murder
81st Murder	82nd Murder	83rd Murder

84th Murder	85th Murder	86th Murder
87th Murder	88th Murder	89th Murder
90th Murder	91st Murder	92nd Murder
93rd Murder	94th Murder	95th Murder
96th Murder	97th Murder	98th Murder
99th Murder	100th Murder	Plus More…

IT AIN'T JUST ABOUT GEORGE FLOYD!!!

All these murders were by the hands of crooked cops. There are many more names, but you get the point. This list does not include those who weren't killed or who endured brutal beatings from cops, but it does contain other ethnicities.

The murders above aren't even a fraction of the lives taken by the hands of those who are supposed to serve and protect. I read the Law Enforcement Oath of Honor, and part of it says they will never betray the trust of the public, and they will hold others accountable for their actions. As we watch the news, scroll through our social media feeds, and listen to the radio, we find they are not upholding their oath (some of them, not all). The corrupt policemen have done the complete opposite. Our trust has been betrayed! Do we expect for all cops to walk in perfection? Of course not, but we do expect them to become one with the oath they've willingly and voluntarily taken. Believe it or not, we want you to make it back home to your family just like we want to make it home to ours. Cops who are racist, power-hungry, power-drunk, or crooked make it hard for the good ones. The straight and narrow law enforcement should be angry with their counterparts who are causing the uproar. The cops who are confident are the ones who do their job and catch a lot of slack doing it, but they serve and protect anyway. I don't care what job you have if you do it with proper training, compassion, wisdom, care, and love, you can still do your job and be tough, if the situation calls for it.

Many say we make everything about racism but fail to recognize the racism that exists. It's aggravating. Then try to justify their claim by posting on their social media handles or bringing up in conversation other cop killings that involved different ethnicities, which is a slap in the face considering how cop killings against the African American community far outweigh others. Sorry. Not sorry. It's not a competition. It's facts. Look at the multitude of police brutality that is caught on camera, but what about those that weren't caught on camera? We are only scratching the surface.

Meanwhile, you say we're always playing the race card. I'm a card player myself, and the main play across any card game is that you can only play the hand you are dealt. You say race card. I say that's what's in our hand. We are looking at the situations right in our face. We know what racism looks like, how it functions, and how it feels, usually because we are always on the blunt end of it. You say you've experienced racism, and you probably have from some black people, and it's wrong. I hope that experience opened your eyes to a glimpse of what we live versus your experience. Also, you may have mistaken racism for our truth. What do I mean by that? During our bold voice conversation, you may feel like it's racism, but it's not; it's our truth that we live every day. I'm sorry it may come across as racist, but we can't lie or hide our reality because it makes you uncomfortable or because of how someone may perceive it; to lie and hide our truth is to not be true to ourselves.

Consequently, due to us enduring racism and constantly fighting to convince people we're not who racists say we are, it's hard to trust because we don't know if you're really hiding how you feel about us (hence my letter to my "friends"). My family and I used to go to a predominantly white church. Our children loved the youth ministry…at first. When our boys became older teens, they started to recognize and experience racism amongst their peers and adults. They told us about it, and as a responsible parent, I went to the youth pastor over the ministry; mind you, I wasn't belligerent or loud. I spoke calmly and articulated my problem reasonably. I was appalled at her reply. She literally said there was nothing she could do as far as the students. She could talk to the teachers, but she couldn't address it with the youth. Her tone, her demeanor, showed she didn't care and wasn't going to do anything about it either way (and she didn't). It was never addressed. Here it is we entrust our children with the youth-adult staff, and she didn't care for her black students. We weren't the right color for her to care.

At that point, I pulled both my boys from the youth ministry because I refused to entrust them with my greatest treasures. Later, I spoke with another adult youth pastor, and he cared about what happened and did everything to welcome my boys back into the fold, and they became part of the ministry again.

Another example we can look at is when Kaepernick kneeled peacefully to protest. He wasn't argumentative or pugnacious, shoot, he wasn't even aggressive, and the same ones that cheered him on and played side-by-side with him, are the same ones who turned against him. I'm sure he was hurt by the betrayal. Here it is as a black man trying to get people to understand his heart and desire for change and did it peacefully. He was crucified for it by those who he thought loved him or at least who he thought would understand. He and others were told they can't do that, but now the African American community has erupted, they wish they allowed him to protest his way. You can't continue to tell us how when you won't listen!

Take a look at this scenario; a nine-year-old white boy comes home and tells you, his parents, that he's being bullied at school by two nine-year-old black boys. You go to the school principal, and nothing is done. The administration won't give the other children's names because of privacy and protection. The bullying continues week after week, month after month, and still, nothing is done about it. You went to the school board, and they reprimand the bullies with a slap on the wrist. When the bullies return to school, the bullying becomes worse. Meanwhile, your child has voiced what he's going through, following all the rules. He's secretly told you the names of the bullies, but you don't know anything about them, so you can't speak with the parents. As the bullying persists, your child falls deeper and deeper into depression, fear grips him, and he no longer wants to attend school. No one from the outside is hearing him. No one from school is listening to him and he's fed up. His emotions are running rampant on the inside, and they are beginning to manifest, emotions spewing out in anger, sadness, misery, hopelessness, and despair. He's deciding two things; does he go and shoot up the school, or does he commit suicide? He has tried to tell you in his own way what he's battling with, but even you still don't get, or you do get it but are weary yourself. Then, one day you come to find that your son hung himself. Now you're sad and in despair and mad as hell. You want justice for your child but can't receive it because the bullies never physically told him to kill himself, and you can't physically prove they were the reasons behind it. Tell me, how do you feel? Those black boys are still walking around and probably bullying someone else. The bullying goes unchecked. You win a civil lawsuit against the school system, but you're still without your child. There isn't enough money that can wipe your tears away because every time you spend a dollar, you think of your child. You can't hug those dollars and feel the warmth and love of your child. You can't kiss those dollars and watch the smile come on those dollar's faces. Those dollars can't walk across the stage as you watch and celebrate its accomplishments. You can't take those dollars out for ice cream, and when the money gets older, it can't have kids of its own. That money can't give you grandchildren. Tell me, how do you feel? Yeah...well, that has been us even after slavery was abolished.

Keisha Y. Lapsley

So, no, this isn't just about George Floyd, he is just the "Ain't No Way We Can Let This Continue!"

Fight for Breonna Taylor!

Arrest her murderers right now!

Sayings & Explanations

I didn't know what title to give this piece

With so much going on it's messing with my peace

The first saying we seem to always hear "Get over it! We didn't enslave you. That's in the past."

Hold up. Wait a minute. Stop accelerating and get your foot off the gas

Just get over it, I'm not sure what you mean

Get off that privileged tit cause it's time for you to wean…

Wean yourself off the self-righteous attitude

You tired of hearing it and we're tired of living it too

Let's do the math

And walk down this 400 plus year path

Put slavery on one side of the balance scale

Then put the racism we still face on the other side of the scale

Then add the bitter seasoning of racism

And the persecution of our peaceful activism

It's hard to forget something that still exists

Yet want us to never forget 911, now there's a plot twist

I guess we should just forget racial profiling too

Or the hateful words and actions some people spew

Should we forget the unlawful killing of our black men and women by police

Or our obvious voter suppression to keep our voices from speaking

You want us to forget an era that still impacts our living circumstances to date

Land stolen, businesses burned, homes torn apart & lynched at an alarming rate

Don't forget the school to prison pipeline

Created to keep us working for free and your pockets aligned

How about making it a crime and doing jail time for being addicted to a chemical substance

Yet for the same thing, y'all get mental health help in abundance

Please tell us again why we should just get over it cause it's in the past

Saying that is the same thing as telling someone to kiss yo' aaaa...

...And another thing that's always said

I have black family and friends well let's gone head and put that to bed

Black family and black friends that may very well be

But all it takes is the right kind of pressure to be applied then we shall see

Sayings & Explanations

Instead of walking around using them as your, I'm not racist trophies

Take up your offering of action, put it on the altar then we'll see if you're revealed as phonies

Show it don't tell it is what we say

Put your money where your mouth is and then maybe our view will sway

Here's a saying, don't let them divide us but it's not them that's doing that

It's your words and your actions and your blindness to see our struggles chitchat

You voice your opinion with closed eyes

Diminishing and drowning out our weary cries

So yes, you get our angry side

Because no matter the right we do a vicious narrative is supplied

Which in turn brings on the next saying, I don't know why they're so angry

Dawg, if you had to fight for everything, you'd be cranky

Do you realize what we have to fight for?

While you get to casually walk through, we have to beat down the doors

We got to fight for equality, justice, employment, laws, the judicial system

Even discrimination, appropriate pay, our own neighborhoods, and racism

There is even more than that in which we fight

You will read this and still be filled with spite

And oh my Gawd! This saying takes me to a whole notha place

"They're animals! They're violent! They're thugs!" shouting this but turn their eyes away from their own race

Who was it that created these "animals"?

Looking back through history as far as slavery even up to today, I'd say your words are fallible

Emmett Till, Selma March, Black Wallstreet, Rodney King, the Central Park Five

Now, try to clear that mental picture off your hard drive

Then we have the assassinations of Malcom X, Fred Hampton, and Martin Luther King

That ain't even a drop in the bucket, but Imma stop pulling at them strings

So, no matter the explanation

You still align and hold the same views as the white supremacist and Aryan nation

NO MO' EXPLANIN'

I Will Not Fear

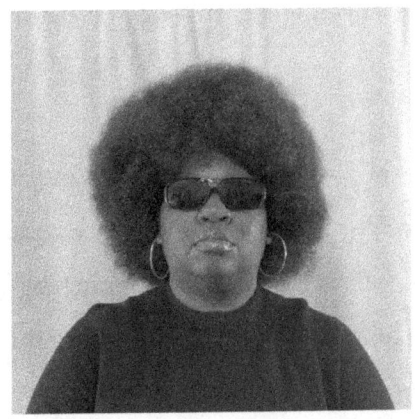

"We fear for our lives!" says some of the picket signs on the protest front lines. At one time, I'd have that same sign too, but my mindset has changed. Fear is a tactic that is designed to immobilize and cower down people and a movement. It's a method that's been used for centuries, and I'm sure it will continue for centuries to come.

Fear: an unpleasant emotion caused by the belief that someone or something is dangerous, likely to cause pain or a threat.

Faith: complete trust or confidence in someone or something

During slavery, masters used fear to immobilize slaves. The tools they used to do it were: whips, amputations, murder, box (also known as sweatbox), attack dogs, and other tactics. The tools used against African Americans today by law enforcement are brutality, death threats if you tell on them or try to prosecute them, murder, incarceration, threatening your family members, beatings, attack dogs, rubber bullets, tear gas, false reports, evidence planting, lies…is there anything I'm missing, or is that enough?

Criminals intimidate witnesses not to snitch on them, and if caught, they are charged with a felony. Police do the exact same thing! Law enforcement builds their cases on people "snitching" but won't apply that same maneuver when it comes to the corrupt cops committing crimes right next to them.

Have you wondered why law enforcement is under such scrutiny? It's because they are trained authority figures who are supposed to uphold the law, live by it, and serve to protect. However, some (not all) have perverted their authority to justify their own means, to fit their agenda, and to serve their own beliefs and ideologies all at the expense of black people. Let me be clear about this though, police brutality knows no color bounds, BUT the unjust killing of African Americans far outweighs the other cultures. Also, I want this to be understood as well; we are not saying we shouldn't go to jail if we commit a crime but what we are saying is we shouldn't have to arrive at a jail cell beat up so severely our face can't be recognized and with broken bones, or not arriving at a prison or home because we were killed unjustly, or dying in police custody. We can be taken into police custody without a scratch, just like it is done for white people.

I'm reminded of a standoff in 2016 between a group of armed white men and police. They occupied a wildlife refuge from January 2, 2016, until February 11, 2016, a little over a whole entire month. One was shot and killed due to reaching for a handgun that he had on him and another one was wounded. Now get this…unbelievable…six of them were sentenced to one to two years' probation and house arrest, seven were acquitted of ALL federal charges, others were convicted with as less as one year in jail, up to three years with probation or time served. I went as far as to check out their mugshots, and you know what I saw? The mugshots of the perps were bruise and scratched free, shoot, even one of them was smiling. Law enforcement was patient (I'm just saying a whole month) and apparently lenient with those "thugs" (as we are called). Please explain to me how they can gather weapons, food, fuel, and other essentials, all the while taking over an entire refuge government facility without being murdered and or brutality beaten by the police. AND! AND! President Trump pardoned the arsonists (who the militia was fighting for) in 2018. Please, please, please tell me, how is that possible? I'll say to you, white privilege! There is absolutely no way black people would have received that type of patience, a whole six weeks! There wouldn't be one black person alive, and in the event, a few did survive, they would have been tried, convicted, and thrown away for more than a decade per person. That is just one example of many. I don't know how much more you need to see to understand white privilege. What's more, I've seen white males with weapons taken into custody without a scratch on them, but we can be empty-handed, complying, and talking trash and are savagely beaten for it and killed.

Be Careful Dear #UrRacismIsShowing

Those people are monsters!

Be Careful Dear #UrRacismIsShowing

You're mad because we're fighting for justice

Be Careful Dear #UrRacismIsShowing

You throw #BlueLivesMatter in our face when taking a stand against the corrupt police

Be Careful Dear #UrRacismIsShowing

We say, #BlackLivesMatter! Then you retort with #AllLivesMatter

Be Careful Dear #UrRacismIsShowing

We can't have a barbeque in the park without you calling the police on us

Be Careful "Karen" #UrRacismIsShowing

Black folk can't do their job and deliver packages without police being called

Be Careful Dear #UrRacismIsShowing

Black kids can't sell water without you calling the cops

Be Careful Dear #UrRacismIsShowing

When we hear, "If you don't like it here, then go back to Africa!"

Be Careful Dear #UrRacismIsShowing

Keisha Y. Lapsley

I am sick of "these" people

Be Careful Dear #UrRacismIsShowing

"Those" people are terrorists

Be Careful Dear #UrRacismIsShowing

When a black man or woman are unjustly killed by the police, and you're silent

Be Careful Dear #UrRacismIsShowing

When the KKK can march peacefully but not BLM

Be Careful Dear #UrRacismIsShowing

When you take from our culture and don't credit us then bounce when trouble comes

Be Careful Dear #UrRacismIsShowing

When our culture is good enough for your use, but you don't stand up from the culture you take from

Be Careful Dear #UrRacismIsShowing

8:46 with your knee on somebody's neck

Be Careful Dear #UrRacismIsShowing

Spit at us then says N*****

NOW YOU KNOW #UrRacismIsShowing

FIGHT FOR BREONNA TAYLOR! SHE'S NOT HERE TO FIGHT FOR HERSELF! ARREST AND CHARGE THE COPS RESPONSIBLE FOR HER DEATH!

Stop Lying!!!

STOP LYING on us saying we're resisting arrest while you twist our arms, having dogs attack us, tasing us without cause, putting us in chokeholds, having your knee on our necks, your full body weight lying on top of us while you're handcuffing us, and shooting us. STOP LYING on us saying you fear for your lives! How can that be when you definitely have enough faith in your badge to commit unlawful crimes? You don't fear us in the way you'd like us to believe. You fear what we can become. You fear our knowledge. You fear our history. You fear us becoming aware of who we were before slavery. You fear being outnumbered. It's just like in the Bible, when Pharaoh feared the growth of the Hebrews, he commanded all the newborns to be killed. You also want to inject fear into our culture. Congratulations! It worked! But you're treading in dangerous waters because we are to the point where we're no longer living in fear. We are coming for you! Through the justice system and the Supreme Court, and that is just the beginning! You took it a step too far. The thing about fear, it only lasts a while, but eventually people grow tired then that brings on a whole other set of problems...as you see!

God taught me something; He showed me that I, no, we can't walk in fear. We can't and won't walk in fear of the possibility of something happening to our sons and daughters, to our husbands and wives, to our sisters and brothers, to our mothers and fathers, and to our family and friends. Fear pulls the subject into the oppressor's atmosphere. It makes us feel how they want us to feel and how they want us to move. Instead, we must walk in faith. We have to trust in our voices. We must trust in our power. We must trust in our knowledge and education. We must trust in God!

Proverbs 6:32 says, "He who is slow to anger is better than the mighty, And he who rules his spirit than he who takes a city."

They are banking on us to cut up and act out in a cop situation. Yes, be angry, but be wise. My husband and I love comic movies and television shows. We love the movie Dark Knight. Our favorite character is the Joker. Depending on the villain, we usually like them better. The heroes do a lot of reacting, but the villains plan and execute strategically. Yes, of course, the heroes come out as winners, barely. They wait for stuff to happen versus being proactive.

Meanwhile, the villains are patient and calculated. Why did I say this? I said it because, in the movies, some of the best villains you love to hate, or revenge storylines are the ones who patiently plotted and implemented their plans advantageously. WE ARE NOT THE VILLAINS! But we do have to reflect, plan, then perform the scheme.

When we live and walk in fear, we're not able to control our anger or take a city. That's what I'm loving about the protests that are happening as we speak! We're not only on the frontlines protesting, but we're protesting by voting, joining, and volunteering with organizations that help our movement, signing petitions, educating ourselves, calling out racism, and many other ways!

Also, we must take into account that these things are going to take time, so we must be patient (about what we can be patient about because some things need immediate attention such as the Aubrey case, Floyd case, Taylor case, and the Reed case). Letting go of fear will allow us to continue to become what we need in our community, such as psychologists (especially male), lawyers, activists, judges, law enforcement, senators, congressmen, mayors, governors, district attorneys, CEOs, sheriffs, teachers, professors, principles, police chiefs, vice presidents, community leaders, generals, president, doctors, and nurses, and any other field that holds a seat of influence.

WE DESERVE A FUTURE!

OUR CHILDREN DESERVE A FUTURE!

AND WE ARE GOING TO GET IT TO THEM!

Keisha Y. Lapsley

Story Time

A wealthy man, by the name of Mali, worked hard to provide for his family. He had the same status as a King. He ran the family business. His grandfather passed on, but he continued to work side by side with his father. Mali's father was getting up in age, though, so he helped more behind the scenes. He was an inventor and harvested and traded gold. He owned land where various minerals were mined. Mali's inheritance was sure to take care of his family and his people for centuries to come. His family had long money, generational wealth.

Mali was married to a beautiful, smart, and educated woman named Sahara. They have two children and another on the way. Sahara taught her children their history, math, science, medicine, and the common knowledge they needed to take care of themselves when they get older. Two of their children were elementary school-aged and middle school-aged. Their middle-school-aged son, Benin, would help with the family business after Sahara released him from learning for the day. Their elementary school-aged daughter, Ghana, would help her mother cook, clean, read books, and always asked her mother questions. She was an inquisitive child.

After a few months, the time came for Sahara to have the baby. The midwife came to their home and helped deliver the baby. This delivery was a little more difficult for Sahara, but she pushed through anyway. They named their baby boy, King. Sahara couldn't do too much because she was sick after having King. The maid helped her a lot and moved in with the family. Ghana was as helpful as she could be when it came to education. She knew her mother couldn't teach her for the time being and took it upon herself to learn reading different books. She made sure her brother Benin would read assigned books to stay sharp.

Meanwhile, over time, Sahara healed, and she was able to go back to doing normal things. While Sahara was taking the time to heal, Mali drew back from working so much. He was concerned about his wife and found it hard to continue to work long hours. He was in a dilemma.

One day, a friend introduced him to a business contact named Brit. He presented Mali with a business proposition that was sure to give him the relief he needed to take care of Sahara while still making money in the process. They worked together for years. Mali invited him to the house for dinner with the family, and he went to Brit's home as well. They became good friends and did a lot of business for one another.

Brit approached Mali one evening, wanting to amend their business venture. He talked it over with his father and Sahara. They were against it because it would mean Brit and his people would have more control over the business. Ghana overheard her parent's conversation. She's now middle-school-aged and smart as a whip. While they slept, she searched for and found the past business contracts and the new business proposition. She ran the numbers and glanced through the past business deals and realized Brit schemed money off the top from the beginning. The next morning while they ate breakfast, Ghana shared what she found. Mali was livid because he trusted Brit. It was then he realized Brit was after more land, and previous conversations he had with him started to make sense.

Simultaneously, across the way, Brit was making plans of his own with his buddies in the event Mali turned down the proposal. He calculated all the moves he needed to make to accomplish what he set out to do. He saw how rich Mali was and was jealous he didn't have that amount. He wanted what Mali had, and it didn't bother him to betray Mali. He never cared for him in the first place.

Later that evening, Mali met Brit at the mines to talk about his new amendment. Mali told Brit that he was completely satisfied with the way things were right now. Brit kept calm and told Mali he understood. He didn't put up a fuss or a fight, and that made Mali concerned. He wasn't sure what to make of it. He didn't mention what his daughter, Ghana, found because he was still trying to figure out Brit's angle.

After a week, things went back to normal between the business partners. Mali was still being careful around Brit, and wouldn't let on, but Brit felt there was a difference. Brit hired new workers. They looked different. They didn't look like the miners who presently work for Brit. They even moved differently. Mali wasn't sure and questioned it, but Brit chalked it up to rotation and giving the workers a break. Still, Mali felt like something wasn't right. His father never trusted Brit from the beginning, and he told Mali that even though he agreed to the partnership. When Mali returned home from work for the evening, he told Sahara what happened and how he thinks Brit is up to something. She couldn't believe her ears. The next day, she called Brit's wife to speak with her about what was happening. Mali was unaware of her plans. When they met up, Sahara asked Brit's wife, Ameri', what was going on, but Ameri' acted as if she wasn't knowledgeable about what was happening. She was nonchalant about it and reassured Sahara all was well, and their friends and Brit wouldn't do anything to hurt the relationship. Sahara noticed how "casual" Ameri' was being and didn't trust her word. As soon as Sahara left, Ameri' sent word to her husband. After conversing with Ameri', Brit decided to move more quickly.

The next morning, Mali and his family got up and went about their morning as usual. Benin was almost an adult and looking forward to working the family business with his father. Ghana is almost high-school age in just a few months. King is late elementary school age. Sahara was getting the lessons ready, and Mali left for work.

When he arrived at work, he didn't see any of his workers. He only saw Brit's workers. He asked Brit where his workers were, and Brit told him they didn't want to work for Mali anymore, so he had to bring more of his men for the mines and trade. Mali snapped and told him to quit lying and to tell him the truth! While Mali was giving Brit a piece of his mind, he didn't notice Brit signaling his men. Next thing you know, Mali was knocked to the ground and chained up and thrown into the cargo with his workers. As he screamed, Brit brought Mali's father out in chains, put him before Mali, and put a sword through his body. Brit said, "I get what I want. Your father is too old to do what I need for him to do and where you're going. Oh, and don't worry about that pretty little wife of yours, I got a job for her and your kids." Mali wept.

Concurrently, back at the house, Brit's men captured Mali's family. He separated them. None of them saw each other again. Mali didn't make the trip to the next country. He became ill on the boat, so they tossed him overboard. He drowned in the sea. No burial. No love, just gone. Brit and three of his men took Sahara and raped her to the point she no longer cared about who she was and what her life used to be. Brit's wife, Ameri', was unaware of what her husband did, which is why she praised him and stayed by his side. They sent Benin to Brit's home country. They sent Ghana to another place, and King stayed behind and slaved in the mines.

Whenever they moved the slaves to new places, they erased any trace of their heritage, homeland, family, and inheritance. Mali's family endured excruciating beatings, overworked with no pay, rape, both male and female, and took their ideas, making them their own. The slave owners stole their inheritance and made them build theirs.

After many, many years, they moved King to a new country. He had no idea where he was, nor did he speak their language. He was a young, grown man now and eventually found him a wife, and they had children. When King's slave owner saw how he loved his family, he sold him to another slave owner, after he raped him in front of them. Then the slave owner took their youngest son and killed him in front of his face before sending him off with his new owner all because he tried to fight back. After sending him off, he kept his oldest son and put him in the place of his father.

Slavery and the generational destruction of this family went on for centuries. The family's lineage remained, but they were lost in who they were as decades passed. They tried to build a life after slavery as best they could, but they never felt complete and couldn't get back on their feet. Their lives depicted nothing of their past. Each generation tried to do better than the next, some failed, and some succeeded. The latest generation went through a lot. The father was killed by police before his child was born, and the mother battled mental illness before committing suicide when her son turned three years old. She couldn't get the help she needed because of the poor quality of healthcare. Law enforcement would throw her in jail instead of getting her the help she needed because they didn't see it as a mental illness, they looked upon her as an addict. After her death, social services took the young boy and put him in the system.

Over time, the young boy nicknamed "Woke" went from foster family to foster family feeling lost. No one wanted him. In fact, anyone that crossed him called him an animal, said he'd never amount to anything, and he's nothing. He was always seen as a threat, although he was intelligent; it's just no one saw the need to pull it out of him. He was angry. Woke didn't dress like everyone else. He didn't walk like everyone else and his hair texture was different. Woke had a flair and style of his own, and he wouldn't bow down to anyone who told him to conform to their way of how they thought he should be or live. He didn't ask to be here or born. He had to fight the foster parents of the homes he lived in because they used him as a servant and beat him. He hated it. He felt dumb, and no one took the time to tell him otherwise. When he got to high school, barely passing, a teacher that looked like him, Mr. Knowledge, took a liking to him (in a professional manner), and decided to take him in and adopt him. Woke didn't make it easy, but "Knowledge" wouldn't give up on him. Knowledge was the teacher's nickname.

Knowledge raised Woke and taught him things about himself he never knew. He armed him with information that would change the trajectory of his life. Knowledge knew if he could get him to understand and know and walk in the power of who was created to be, Woke would change the nation. He showed him his heritage. They worked on an ancestry website to find out who he is, so he'd no longer feel or be lost. After much research and studying, Woke's soul started to awaken. He could feel the power of his ancestors speaking to him. The ancestry research showed him he was a descendant of Mali and Sahara, his bloodline. He finally felt connected to something that belonged to him. He learned of his inheritance and his wealthy lineage, but he also became angry after learning what happened to his family. Here he is in a whole other country that doesn't respect him, treats him like trash, will not provide justice for people like him, and refuses to treat him and those like him like a human being. Dog's lives mean more to people than his life. He's awake, and he's mad!

When he became an adult, he led the fight against injustice and still does to this day. The more he'd fight, the more people would come after him and try to discredit his name. Woke was arrested a few times during protests, even though he marched peacefully. People sent hate mail to his house. Most of the letters said the same thing, "If you don't like it here, then go back where you came from." The ignorance of those words infuriated him. They'd rather him go back to a place where land has exchanged hands multiple times, no longer his, knowing nothing of that place, and once again, take him from a place he's always known rather than to confront the sins of their fathers and make a real change for all people. The sad thing about his homeland is some countries are partakers of his properties because of the riches of the land. There's no way to reclaim what was stolen because now it's emerged in world trade, and they aren't going to let that go. Stolen wages, stolen souls, stolen lives, and stolen land built upon the backs, blood, sweat, and tears of the ones who it was stolen from, and they think Woke and his people are supposed to be cool with that. Woke has awakened and so has his people, and they are in it to win it!

I didn't cover all our history in this story because I don't have that much paper. I think you get my gist, though. I want to make this point clear; everything was stolen from us! Our inheritance was taken from us. Our history wiped clean (which is why some information is still debatable). Our lineage distorted, although we're trying to connect to it. Our livelihood was stolen. You talk about African Americans taking your livelihood and complain and moan about it, but you don't address the fact we still don't have ours (to some degree) because it was STOLEN!

Environmentalists talk about, research, and work to protect the environment. They teach us and warn us about the dangers of mistreating the environment. Some of us choose not to listen due to selfishness of our own wants and desires. There is one thing the environmentalists do not cover is the spilled innocent blood of men and women both young and adult.

> **"The LORD said, "What have you done? Listen! Your brother's blood cries out to me from the ground."**
> **– Gen 4:10**

"Innocent blood still speaks."

Of course, this is more of a spiritual metaphor, however, it still carries a necessary weight. Please do not think there aren't any repercussions for the sheading of innocent blood of African American people. Souls are crying out from the grave and they will be heard. What America is experiencing right now on a massive scale are the blood cries from beyond the catacombs and tombs. The wailings and groanings have become so loud they can't be ignored. God won't allow it!

How would you feel if your inheritance were taken from you? How would you feel if you were separated from your wife or husband, never to see them again and not knowing what happened to them? How would you feel if you worked on and owned your business for years, only for someone else to come and take it from you because they want it? How would you feel if your child were taken from you, raped, and hung or beaten and kidnapped? How would you feel? How would you live? Would you be peaceful, or would you be in rage? How would you feel if the same person who raped you and cut off your feet so you can't run continued to make you work for them for free or pennies on the dollar? How would you feel if authority figures came in your house unannounced and started shooting killing your one and only daughter? How would you feel if you had a billion-dollar idea and had investors lined up, only for one of them to steal your idea and sell it as their own and cut you out? Change only works if you're honest with yourself while answering these questions.

We want you to know. We're not slaves; it was what they called us. We are a beautiful people. We don't know where we belong because all that we were was stripped from us. You talk about protecting your land (but it ain't yours), and if we come to your home, you will kill us, yet we were taken from all we knew to become something never designed for us. Who's done more harm? You can't be mad at the "monsters" and "animals" you created. A friend of our family put it beautifully as we spoke on the phone the other day. He, "Dice," said, "We are the children of the oppressors, so if we're animals, where did that behavior derive from? If the children are bad, it's because they had bad parents." It's time to look in the mirror. Look at what was instilled in us by YOU! I wouldn't just say your ancestors because of the systems in place to this day is still governed by YOU! Things must change. Violence is at the core of slavery (both mentally and physically). If you don't want a violent country, then slavery and everything that surrounds it must be uprooted and replaced with fresh soil and new seeds of peace, justice, and equality.

I've explained all that I'm going to explain in this book. I don't mind having conversations with people who want to listen, learn, and grow. If we're going to grow as a country, then we have to talk to one another. However, if you don't want to listen and are angry because we're taking a stand, I'm done! You won't hear another word from me unless you're watching me on television and movies, reading my books, or listening to me on the radio or podcast. Still, I will tell you this, buckle up because we are not done fighting for justice, equality, and respect!

No Mo' Explainin'!

We are done explaining to those who don't want to listen!
Our struggle is so plain to see that you don't even need 20/20 vision
If you want to keep acting like you don't know
Acting as if you haven't read the letter of Jim Crow
Thinking you can call a foul so you can get a free throw
Homeboy, homegirl, apparently you didn't get the memo!
Our train ain't gone stop and change is gone come
You think we lyin' down, but we are far from being done!
I'd suggest you cover your eyes and get some earplugs to cover your eardrums
Because ain't no stoppin' us when we overcome!
We comin' out loud and bold and oh will it be a sight to see
Standing tall and strong like a cedar and an oak tree
And to those who choose to understand and take the educated route
We are more than willing to share our story, so come on over to the cookout!

NOW...

**FIGHT FOR BREONNA TAYLOR!
SHE'S NOT HERE TO FIGHT FOR HERSELF!
ARREST AND CHARGE THE COPS RESPONSIBLE FOR HER DEATH!**

About the Author

Keisha Lapsley is an established author, publisher, writing mentor, screenwriter, and CEO of KeyCity Enterprise. She's the wife of Retired, SFC Douglas Lapsley, and they have three children together. She graduated from Virginia College with a Certification in Culinary Arts in October 2014. She was on the Dean's List and served on the Ambassadors Committee. She's received numerous Awards of Appreciation within the military community. Keisha has served throughout the military community from the various duty stations they were assigned. She mentors new writers how to write then help them to publish their books for the past 13 years. She is the Founder of Warriorfied Women and L.O.R.D. (Ladies of Royalty & Dignity). Keisha has published many books of her own "Homeless: My Favorite Park Bench," The Gift of Helps: Learning When to Say No!", "I Did It Wrong," "Jesus the Janitor," and coaching books called "Hand-crafted," and "Stop Wasting Your Business Dollars" are just a few among them. She has upcoming books coming out by the end of the year, such as "Gem of a Lady," "A Love Worth Waiting For," and "Daniel: The Father's Call." She has upcoming movies and television shows as well.

Contact Information

Website – www.authorklap.com

Email – keycitypro@gmail.com

Other Books by the Author

Homeless: My Favorite Park Bench

The Gift of Helps: Learning When to Say No

I Did It Wrong!

A Woman's Dilemma

Who Said Love Doesn't Hurt?

Upcoming Books This Year & Next Year

Gem of a Lady

A Love Worth Waiting For

Homeless 2: Stained Worship

Homeless 3: Withered Flowers

Daniel's Kingdom: The Father's Call (YA)

I AM A TREE (Children's Book)

We're Alright (Children's Book)

www.ingramcontent.com/pod-product-compliance
Lightning Source LLC
LaVergne TN
LVHW041457070426
835507LV00009B/657